Given to Dan & Susan

MW00893259

/10

COOPER'S PACK ™

LONDON

by kyle & groot

Cooper's Pack Publishing

Cooper's Pack, London is a work of fiction. Any resemblance to real people or animals, stuffed or otherwise, is purely coincidental.

All the animals had fun in the writing of this book.

Copyright © 2008 by kyle & groot / A.R.T

All rights reserved.

ISBN-13: 978-0-9794882-1-4
ISBN-10: 0-9794882-1-4

Library of Congress Control Number: 2008907098

All rights reserved, including the right to reproduce the book or portions thereof in any form whatsoever. No part of Cooper's Pack may be stored, reproduced, or transmitted by any means, electronic, mechanical, photocopying, recording, or otherwise without written permission from the authors.

For user permissions, special discounts for bulk purchases, custom activity books, and/or ancillary information, visit CoopersPack.com or contact Cooper's Pack Publishing at Cooper@CoopersPack.com or 877-278-3278.

Cooper's Pack is a registered trademark of kyle & groot, along with A.R.T.

Printed in U.S.A.

The Secretary of State
of the United States of America
hereby requests all whom it may concern to permit the citizen/
national of the United States named herein to pass
without delay or hindrance and in case of need to
give all lawful aid and protection.

Le Secrétaire d'Etat
des Etats-Unis d'Amérique
prie par les présentes toutes autorités compétentes de laisser passer
le citoyen ou ressortissant des Etats-Unis titulaire du présent passeport,
sans délai ni difficulté et, en cas de besoin, de lui accorder
toute aide et protection légitimes.

SIGNATURE OF BEARER/SIGNATURE DU TITULAIRE/FIRMA DEL TITULAR

COOPER

NOT VALID UNTIL SIGNED

PASSPORT

USA

UNITED STATES OF AMERICA

Type / Type / Tipo   Code / Code / Código   Passport No. / No. du Passeport
P   USA   0150619420

Surname / Nom / Apellidos

Given names / Prénoms / Nombres

Nationality / Nationalité / Nacionalidad
UNITED STATES OF AMERICA

Date of birth / Date de naissance / Fecha de nacimiento
Jun 19

Sex / Sexe / Sexo   Place of birth / Lieu de naissance / Lugar de nacimiento
M

Date of issue / Date de délivrance / Fecha de expedición
06 Feb 2006

Date of expiration / Date d'expiration / Fecha de caducidad
04 Feb 2016

Amendments / Modifications / Enmiendas
See Page 24

Authority / Autorité / Autoridad
Seattle

P<USACO<<OPER<<<<<<<<<<<<<<<<<<<<<<<<<<<
001515387USA151506190<<<<<<<<<<<<<<<<<387<<<<<<<<<<<<<<<06

24

DA-OK

Conf # LOLBFF

Date:
Frequent Flyer Nbr:
E-Ticket Nbr: 02134214209
Flight   AIR 15

Gate: S9

Destination: London, England

Seat: 10-A

BOARDING PASS

I can't believe I'm flying to London.

A few hours ago I was with my buddy Phinney in New York and now I'm off to see the rest of the world.

I ♥ NY

We had a great time in
New York City and I really
appreciated Phinney's travel
advice:

· Have fun and take pictures.
· Be courteous and respectful
  to others.
· Be smart and learn about
  new cultures.
· Make new friends.

As we prepared to land in London, I was glad Phinney arranged for a friend of his to meet me at the airport.

6

I had to look for a lamb
wearing a tie...that would
be his friend L.L..

How many tie-wearing lambs can
there be?

I hope I spot him.

After getting my passport "stamped" for the first time, I walked through Customs and into the Arrivals Hall.

8

I looked high and low, then I looked lower.

There I noticed a little woolly ball holding a sign with my name on it.

That has to be L.L....

Cooper

"I'm Cooper and you must be
L.L.. Nice to meet you. Like
the tie."

"Herrow!" replied L.L.
"Like the *rucksack*."

 Look for local words and
phrases in *italics*.

L.L. asked if I was ready to see London.

"Let's do it!" I replied, wondering how his tie didn't get caught in the escalator.

We headed down to the express trains to start the journey.

On the train into London we
shared stories about my trip
in New York and how L.L.
knows Phinney.

12

L.L. told me he met Phinney years ago at the Woolex Regatta in Hyde Park.

"We've been *mates* ever since," he added.

Paddington Station

Trolley: British for Cart

We soon arrived at Paddington Station (I thought that was the name of a bear?!?) and headed to the **_Cash Point_** (L.L.'s word for ATM) to get some local currency.

Fun Facts:

There is a famous bear named after this station who wears a blue duffle coat and loves orange marmalade.

Paddington Station opened in 1854.

15

With cash in paw, we headed outside to the taxi **queue**.

L.L. told the driver to take us to Covent Garden and off we went...

I couldn't help but notice the driver was sitting on the wrong side of the car.

For that matter, he was driving on the other side of the road.

L.L. laughed, "In England, driving on the left side of the road is **proper.**"

"So left is right and right is wrong?" I said.

"Right," said L.L..

Right.

We arrived at Covent Garden, one of London's famous outdoor markets, and walked around.

Everything seemed a little different from what I was used to.

The phone booths were red and there were street signs on every building.

I even saw a man selling the "World's Smallest Kite".

ROYAL OPERA HOUS

LONDON TRANSPORT MUSEUM

THEATRE MUSEUM

COVENT GARDEN MARKET

TELEPHONE

LAZENBY COURT WC2

CITY OF WESTMINSTER

Westminster? Thought I was in London... 63

"A *holiday* is never complete without a kite," said L.L..

I had to agree so we purchased one and off we went...

 Fun Facts:

The "Garden" was originally a vegetable field in the Middle Ages.

Covent Garden later became London's first public market.

They like lambs here.

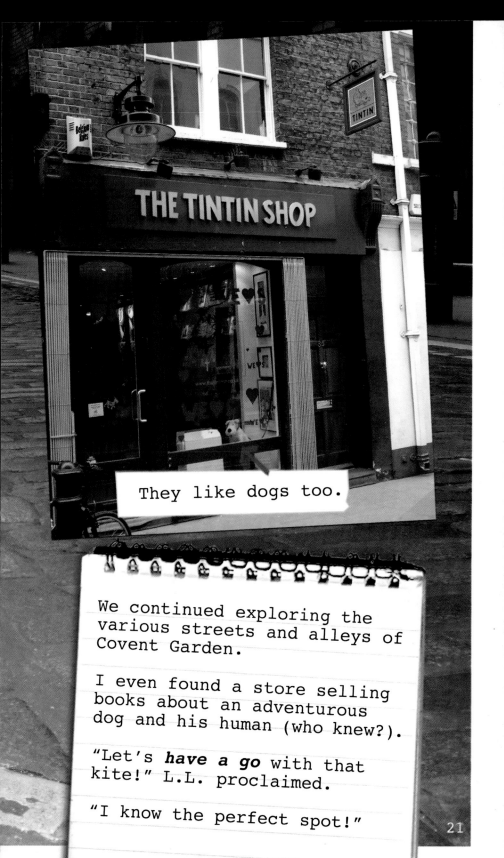

They like dogs too.

We continued exploring the various streets and alleys of Covent Garden.

I even found a store selling books about an adventurous dog and his human (who knew?).

"Let's **have a go** with that kite!" L.L. proclaimed.

"I know the perfect spot!"

After a short walk, we headed through a small archway and entered a large courtyard.

The building was called Somerset House, L.L. explained.

"There is a **lovely** ice rink here in the winter and water fountains coming out of the bricks in the summer," he continued.

Lucky for us, the courtyard was clear.

Up, up and away...

Fun Facts:

Built in 1547 as a private mansion, Somerset House later became a palace for England's royalty.

It is now a center for arts, learning, and government offices.

Check out the river view on the backside of the building!

23

Waterloo Stations ⇌ ⊖

IMAX Cinema

King's College

National Film Theat...

Royal Festival Hall & Hayward Gal...

Thames Path & Bankside

Walking across Waterloo Bridge.

After a little mishap with the kite (bummer), we walked across the **River Thames**.

L.L. said he was taking me to one of the city's largest tourist attractions, the London Eye.

I wasn't sure what the "Eye" was but I definitely wanted to check out that giant Ferris wheel!

We continued along an area called the South Bank and saw some folks covered in paint.

L.L. told me they are called "living statues".

"Spooky" I said, but gave one a **quid** anyways.

To my great fortune, the London Eye was the Ferris wheel I saw earlier (though they call it an observation wheel).

From the ground it looked like the world's largest set of bicycle spokes I had ever seen.

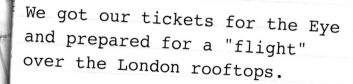

We got our tickets for the Eye and prepared for a "flight" over the London rooftops.

Boarding ➔
gate

Please have your
tickets ready

One ticket per
person

➔

➔

Entering an "Eye-Pod".

There's the bridge we just crossed and Somerset House where I lost my kite!

Wow, you could see the whole city!

L.L. pointed out that his *flat* wasn't far away from **the Gherkin**.

Flat pickles? Hmmm...

 Fun Facts:

The London Eye is 443 feet tall (135 meters), equal to 64 red telephone booths stacked on each other.

It takes about 30 minutes for a full rotation.

The Gherkin, in the City of London.

From the top of the Eye, the busses looked like little toys.

I definitely recommend taking this flight (and you don't even need a seatbelt!).

Big Ben

House of Parliament

Fun Facts:

Parliament is the seat of government for the United Kingdom of Great Britain and Northern Ireland. 63

Parts of the building are over 1,000 years old!

31

We headed across Westminster
Bridge towards one of the
world's most famous landmarks,
Big Ben.

There were people everywhere
taking pictures (or maybe
checking the time?).

Waterloo Stations

Jubilee Gardens

National Arts & Entertainment Centres

Thames Path & Festival Pier

Tower & Bankside

Fun Facts:

Big Ben is the nickname of the Great Bell located in the Clock Tower's belfry.

Ben first rang in 1859.

The tower is 314 feet tall (96 meters).

Our journey continued to Buckingham Palace, The Queen's official home in London. Nice house.

"You can tell if the Queen is home by the type of flag displayed over the palace," said L.L..

Home   Not Home

His hat is fuzzy like Phinney.

Fun Facts:

Buckingham Palace has 775 rooms and 78 bathrooms.

35

Britain's smallest Police Station...no joke!

After the palace, we headed over to Trafalgar Square.

L.L. can really keep up a pace (especially considering his small legs!).

Fun Facts:

Trafalgar Square was built to honor Admiral Lord Nelson's victory at the Battle of Trafalgar in 1805.

Make sure to dodge the pigeons!

Nelson's Column.

During our trek I asked what the initials L.L. meant.

"Little Lambie of course," he replied.

Well that makes sense...

39

We came to an intersection called Piccadilly Circus.

There were electronic and neon signs everywhere, including an **advert** featuring my guide and new friend L.L..

Very cool I thought, but where are the elephants?

BluBerr-E.com

Bluberr-E™

a·r·t

artdart.com

ZOË₂

s.a.

le parfum naturel

esa.com

Fun Facts:

Latin for circle, "circus" refers to a round intersection at a street junction.

You may not see any clowns, but you can still find some *sweets.*

41

We decided to head back to L.L.'s *flat* and call it a day.

His suggestion to take the *Tube* (London's underground rail system) was well received.

Once again, now we're talking, no more walking!

Fun Facts:

London's first subway system was opened in 1890.

There are now 11 separate lines carrying over 28 million people each year.

For obvious reasons, L.L. doesn't use the *Tube* much.

He likes taxi cabs (they'll pick him up).

43

L.L.'s **flat** was **the bee's knees.**

What a Top Dog day we had!

45

We popped out early the next morning for a **spot of tea** near the Tower of London.

L.L. said the Tower was London's most infamous prison for famous people.

These days it is a **fabulous** spot for furry dogs (and fluffy lambs).

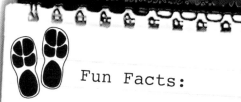 Fun Facts:

The Tower of London originates from the 1080's when William the Conqueror built a stone tower inside his wooden fortress.

It used to have a zoo with leopards, an elephant, and even a polar bear (which was kept on a chain and allowed to catch fish in the Thames...how cool is that?!?).

My time in London was almost over.

Although I was sad to be leaving, I had a train to catch for my next destination.

I thanked L.L. for the great tour of London.

I know I will see him again (at least on a tv commercial or billboard).

L.L. wished me well and said goodbye.

I had a new friend in the world and you can never go wrong with that.

Off to my next adventure ...*brilliant!*

Mount Rainier.

View of Seattle from the Space Needle.

Hanging on the water.

Seattle is in the state of Washington.

My collection of toy planes.

There is a mini Statue of Liberty near my house!

More to Explore:

Create a scrapbook showing your hometown and favorite things to do!

After your travels, see if your favorite activities have changed.

COOPER'S PACK
LONDON

51

More to Explore:

Locate a world map and compare the size of different countries in the world.

How large is Mexico compared to Morocco?

How many Iceland's can you fit in India?

Are Bolivia and Botswana the same size?

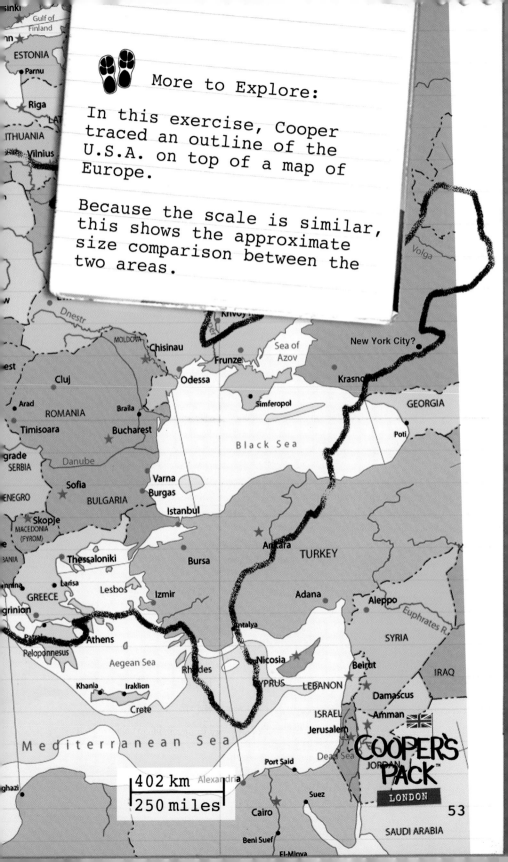

More to Explore:

In this exercise, Cooper traced an outline of the U.S.A. on top of a map of Europe.

Because the scale is similar, this shows the approximate size comparison between the two areas.

COOPER'S PACK
LONDON

Tips on Pronunciation:

River Thames = Tems / Temz
Aluminium = Al-yoo-min-i-um
Vitamins = V(it)-a-mins
Schedule - (ssh)e-dule
Leisure - Le-zure
Fillet = Fil-it

Even though it is all English, some words are spelled slightly different...

centre - center
theatre - theater
colour - color
grey - gray
flavour - flavor
programme - program
metre - meter

What do they mean when they say...

Cheers - Thank You
Posh - Very Elegant
Spot on - Exactly right
Have a go - Take a turn
Bob's your uncle - Matter of fact
Jumble sale - Garage sale
Kip - Sleep
CV - Résumé

U.K.		U.S.A.
Biscuits	-	Cookies
Trainers	-	Tennis Shoe
Lorrie	-	Truck
Flat	-	Apartment
Rubbage	-	Garbage
Boot	-	Trunk (of car)
Jumper	-	Sweater
Football	-	Soccer
Mate	-	Friend
WC	-	Bathroom
Trolley	-	Cart

li was here

The Orange Boar
Public House
20 08

Oh yeah, *Nosh* (food).

The Orange Boar
Public House

Black Pudding — £5.5
Our classic sausage made from cow blood served with freash bread.

Bangers & Mash — £8.5
Our famous sausage and mashed potatos with onion gravy all over.

Bubble & Squeak
Our special recipe sausage, p... and fresh vegetables in a fry-up...

Shepherd's Pie — £9.0
Our seasoned ground mutton and vegetables topped off with mashed potatoes and cheese, baked to a bubbling golden brown.

Fish & Chips
A fresh fillet of Cod coated in our house recipe beer batter, fried to a crisp and served with natural cut potatoes.

All items above served with mushy peas upon request.

Baked Beans on Toast — £1.0
Kind of says it all.

Orange, Public Hous

High Tea

Choice Tea
Plain and Golden Raisin Sco...
Clotted Cream
and
Ferguson's Fabulous Flavou...
with
... Tarts
... selection of
Homemade
...lad, Cream Cheese, Waterc...
...mato and Cucumber
... Sandwiches
...ariety of
...Pastries

Fun Facts:

The British often have *High Tea* in the afternoon, which started out as a light snack between the mid-day meal and supper.

COOPER'S PACK
LONDON

Some currency used in the United Kingdom:

£2.00
Two Pounds
Sterling

20p
Twenty Pence

£1.00
One Pound
Sterling
(Quid)

10p
Ten Pence

50p
Fifty Pence

2p
Two Pence

1p
One Penny

£20.00
Twenty Pounds
Sterling

£10.00
Ten Pounds
Sterling

£5.00
Five Pounds
Sterling

story   Bookmarks   Window   Help
www.cooperspack.com/playground
per NYC   Cooper London   Bluberr-E (TM)   Crumpet Live   Ferguson's Flavours   whizz.com   Woolex Watches   zoé parfum
Coopers Adventure.swf
Q~ Whizz Ed Exchange Rate Exercis

COOPER'S PACK
ADVENTURES

Good work. $5 is 820 Hungarian Forints.

Exchange rate
$1 = 164
Hungarian Forints

whizz

This item costs $5

820 Hungarian Forints

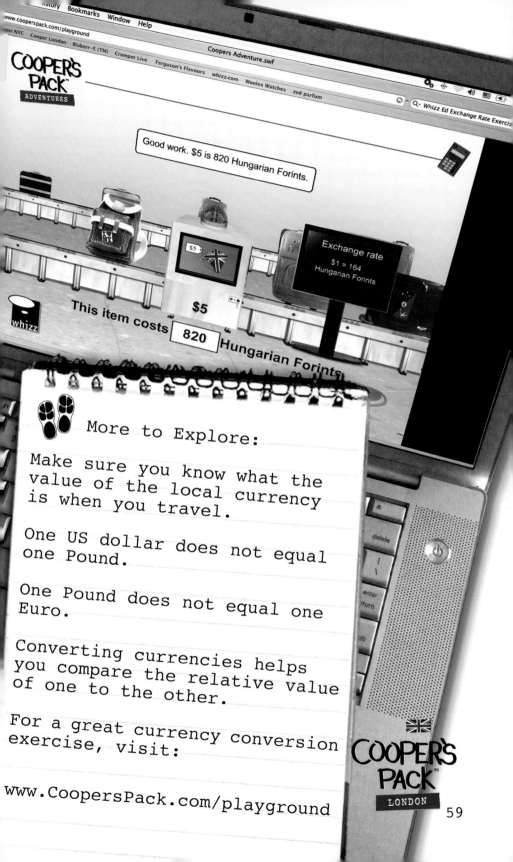

More to Explore:

Make sure you know what the value of the local currency is when you travel.

One US dollar does not equal one Pound.

One Pound does not equal one Euro.

Converting currencies helps you compare the relative value of one to the other.

For a great currency conversion exercise, visit:

www.CoopersPack.com/playground

COOPER'S PACK
LONDON

Places I visited:

Covent Garden
Somerset House
London Eye
Buckingham Palace
Trafalgar Square

Other places to see...

British Museum
Tate Modern
National Gallery
British Library
Regent's Park
Camden Market
Westminster Abbey
Harrods Toy Department
Natural History Museum
Kensington Gardens
Hyde Park

Regent's Park

Paddington Station

Somerset House

Waterloo Bridge

Piccadilly Circus

Hyde Park

Trafalgar Square

The E

Buckingham Palace

Big Ben

City of London

Tower Bridge

More to Explore:

Draw a map of all the places you visited and the things you saw.

COOPER'S PACK
LONDON

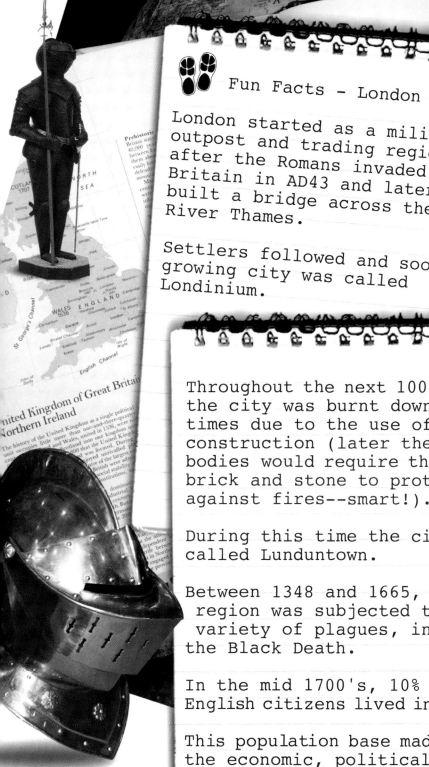

Fun Facts - London

London started as a military outpost and trading region after the Romans invaded Britain in AD43 and later built a bridge across the River Thames.

Settlers followed and soon the growing city was called Londinium.

Throughout the next 1000 years, the city was burnt down many times due to the use of wood construction (later the ruling bodies would require the use of brick and stone to protect against fires--smart!).

During this time the city was called Lunduntown.

Between 1348 and 1665, the region was subjected to a variety of plagues, including the Black Death.

In the mid 1700's, 10% of all English citizens lived in London.

This population base made London the economic, political, and cultural center of England.

By the late 1800's, London's population was over 3,000,000 people!

It now has more than 8,000,000 inhabitants, speaking over 300 different languages.

Greater London includes the City of London, the City of Westminster, and several boroughs such as Camden, Hackney, Lambeth, and Greenwich.

London is the capital city of the United Kingdom's government.

The constitutional monarchy is composed of the House of Lords (inherited landowners) and the House of Commons (elected by the public).

The government's leader is called the Prime Minister (not the president!).

Cooper's Pack
LONDON

63

His hair is longer than groot's.

Royal Mail Post Box.

"*Colourful*" characters.

More to Explore:

Take a variety of pictures showing where you visited.

Always remember the art!

South Bank.

Gates to Green Park.

Looking for something clever.

COOPER'S PACK
LONDON

Double Decker Bus.

Overland Rail Train.

Licensed Cab.

Mail Van.

River Boat.

Work Van.

More to Explore:

How does London get around?

COOPER'S PACK
LONDON

67

Name: Cooper
Height: 6"
Weight: 8oz
Eye Color: Black
Born: Olympic Mountains
(outside of Seattle, WA)

Favorites:

Foods: T-bone steak, milk
Color: Navy blue
Places: Hiking, Pacific Ocean,
        Grandpa's house
Books: 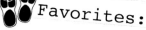A Separate Peace
Artist: Marcus Bausch, Jr.
Teacher: Mr. Axling(Geography)
Class: Geography
Music: Phish, Pete Droge
Sports: Soccer, skiing,
        hackysack, boating
Hobbies: Map collecting
Sayings: "Top Dog"
Nicknames: Coop

Name: L.L. Ferguson
Height: 3"
Weight: 4 oz
Eye Color: Black
Born: Tackley, Oxfordshire
(A nice place in England)

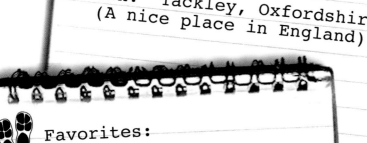 Favorites:

Foods: Bangers & mash, chips
Color: British racing green
Places: Warwick Castle,
        London at night
Books: Tin Tin
Teacher: Mrs. M. Ferguson
Class: Geography
Music: Billy Bragg, Coldplay
Sports: Football, tennis,
        bouldering
Hobbies: Traveling,
         collecting books,
         playing the piano
Sayings: "Herrow?"
Nicknames: Tumshie

COOPER'S
PACK
LONDON

Insert your photo here.

Name: _____

Height: _____

Weight: _____

Eye Color: _____

Born: _____

Languages: _____

Favorites:

Places: _____

Books: _____

Music: _____

Sayings: _____

Nickname: _____

Insert photo of your traveling buddy or the city you visited here.

Travel Information:

Date: _____

Destination(s): _____

_____

_____

Transportation: _____

_____

_____

 More to Explore:

Record your travels, including the places you saw and the people you met.

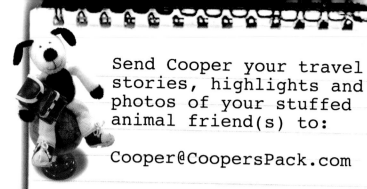

Send Cooper your travel stories, highlights and photos of your stuffed animal friend(s) to:

Cooper@CoopersPack.com

You may find them featured on Cooper's website, including updates and additional pictures of Cooper's adventures.

Photography Credits:

Steve Walker : Page 6
(Chobham, England)

Siobhan McKeering : Pages 8-9
(Dublin, Ireland)

Math Tutorials:

Whizz Education Inc. : P. 58-59

 www.Whizz.com

 kyle

Floating around
the world and
meeting new people.

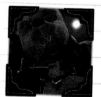 groot

Loves the piano
and creating
fauxtographs.